The first task when embarking on a challenge such as this is to choose a suitable piece of wood that will match our requirements.

This was not easy, for unlike our previous spoons this piece had to be a rather large size. The wood that was selected was a piece of ash, common to the area of Pembrokeshire, where we live. The next stage was to plan what would actually be recorded on the spoon. With this set, work began, but it was not long before we realised that the wood had suffered water damage. We tried to persevere with it, but the damage was so great that the task was impossible. So we turned our attentions to a piece of sycamore, again a local timber which is common in the area, only to find that this too was unsuitable because of staining caused by poor seasoning. This made us stop and think. So often in life we set out to achieve something and obstacles stand in our way. At this point we could have returned to our comfort zone and satisfied ourselves that we had set ourselves an impossible task. It was better to have tried and failed than not to have tried at all. Then my son made a suggestion, "Why don't you use oak?" Previously I had dismissed this idea because I thought that the timber would be too hard to work. With his encouragement we began our search for another suitable piece of timber. We found a piece of Welsh oak from the Gwaun Valley. The journey had begun, little acorns to mighty oaks - we hoped!

3

The woodcarver's interest in carving began during his apprenticeship as a carpenter.

He first heard about the tradition of lovespoon making on the day of the Investiture of Prince Charles in 1969 and made his first simple spoon, (hoping to save having to buy an engagement ring!) Despite being simple it is authentic, as it was actually given and accepted as a token of engagement.

engagemen

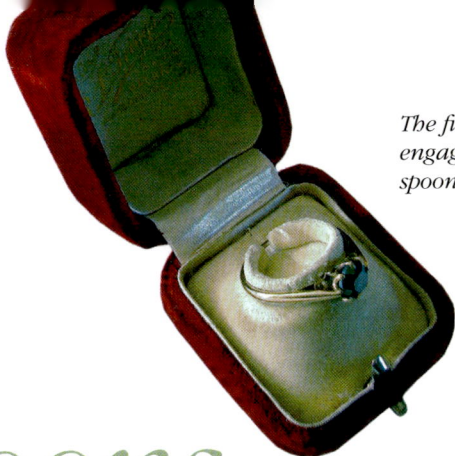

The first engagement spoon, 1969.

poons

The second year of the engagement in 1970 was recorded with a more elaborate design. A simple story of love and the hope of setting up home together.

1970

ICH DIEN

Also shown are a variety of spoons suitable for engagements. The bowl of the spoon is a representation of mixing and blending two hearts together.

A lovespoon is often presented to the bride on her wedding day. This is sometimes the task of a flower girl.

The 1971 wedding spoon took almost a hundred hours to complete and includes appropriate symbolism, including bells, hearts and horseshoes. There are four bowls at the base, two rough and two smooth, (for the rough and smooth of married life.) An issue for debate! Other spoons fitting for a wedding are also featured.

wedding spoons

Flowers: the hope that love will blossom.

anniversary spoons

The symbol for the first anniversary is paper, in Welsh it is priodas papur.

2nd	cotton
3rd	leather
4th	fruit/flowers
5th	wooden
6th	sugar/iron
7th	wool/copper
8th	pottery/bronze

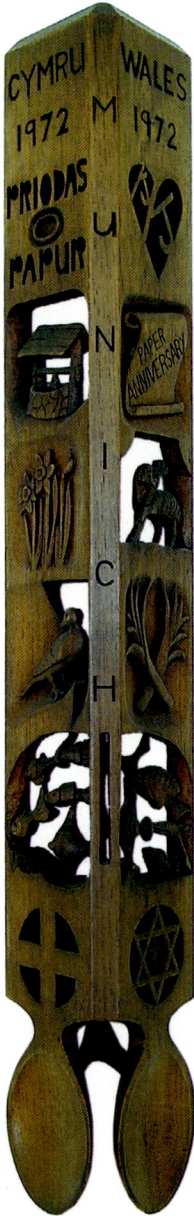

Lovespoons are popular gifts for recording wedding anniversaries.

9th .... willow

10th .... tin

11th ....steel

12th .... silk/linen

13th ....lace

14th .... ivory

15th ....crystal

20th .... china

9

The colour of wood can also reflect the anniversary e.g. mahogany for ruby, oak for golden.

25th		silver
30th		pearl
35th		coral
40th		ruby
45th		sapphire
50th		golden
55th		emerald
60th		diamond

10

tools of the trade

The Longest Lovespoon

The design of the spoon takes the form of eight panels joined together with seven links. The idea was taken from our 2006 spoon, which linked two spoons made from one piece of wood.

12" ruler shown in proportion for scale.

The theme of the spoon is a journey.

Travel and destinations are very much issues that our society finds fascinating. We use all sorts of methods to help us with directions - maps, satellites, computers and of course the compass. However, returning to our theme of the journey we included a compass with a statement inside a heart - "You are here" a phrase frequently used on town maps.

The reason for this was to pose the question "Where are you on your journey?" At the top, the chalice is neither half full nor half empty but over-flowing as stated in Psalm 23. The fluid from the chalice flows continuously throughout the spoon which is shown with tiny droplets.

The spoon is in excess of 27' feet long, however the a

expressions
of faith

Churches and cathedrals throughout the world are full of woodcarvings with religious images. It is not surprising then, that symbols of faith have made their way into the tradition of lovespoon making.

We are constantly presented with choices as to the direction we shall take in life.

There are many journeys, some spiritual some physical. The church starts its journey at the beginning of Advent and travels throughout the year learning from the life of Jesus. Physical journeys take man forms. On life's journey we need to be prepared, for whatever situation we find ourselves in. To cope with life's unpredictable journeys a sense of humour is good to have. With this in min third panel from the top is all about some of the amusing in that have happened in our workplace.

Throughout our lives music plays a big part in all sorts of forms. Music is a medium which can change moods and fill our senses in an extraordinary way, unlike any other subject enriching our lives making the world a better place.

On one particular occasion, my son was convinced that he had seen a mouse near a woodpile. He went into the shed to investigate; just as he was peering underneath the planks his mobile phone rang, vibrating in his pocket. He nearly hit the roof and we never did see the mouse!

tual length is not as important as the message it portrays.

Bells
announcing a
wedding or
celebration.

Flowers -
The hope that
love will blossom.

Swans - Partner
for life.

The wheel -
I will work
for you.

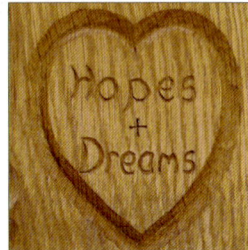

Key to your
heart.

Hopes
& Dreams.

We hear much about leading a balanced life and recreation being good for us. Symbols for sport, leisure and the building blocks of education are all depicted on the spoon. In order for fulfilment, man needs to work, to symbolise this we have the tools of industry and different professions.

Seeds are the traditional symbol of children and are carved above the spoon, with the statement Hopes and Dreams important in all of our lives.

Creation itself is full of a variety of colour, sound and beauty for us to behold. One of the panels is used to show the wonder of creation with carvings of birds, bees, butterflies and flowers.

Finally a well is placed right at the bottom representing the well of living water that is eternally sustained.

Oak leaf and acorn -
The hope that love
will grow big
and strong.

The harp
for the music
of love.

The train
symbolises travel.

Wars are
poor chisels
for carving
out peace.

Beehive -
Hoping love will
always be sweet.

Love birds -
Togetherness.

Lovespoons *with messages*

Good and evil

This spoon demonstrates the struggle between good and evil. Showing a dragon driving a spear through a shield into the heart, like a lightning strike. The sword with the word hope is driven through the dragon. In times of trouble there is still hope through Christ.

Thanks to God

At the base of the spoon, the hands of a child form the shape of a begging bowl. This then develops into a seed giving rise to a sheaf of corn, showing that we are thankful to God for the food in the world. There is enough for everyone, if only it was shared.

Grace

- God's
- Riches
- Available in
- Christ for
- Everyone

On the one side of the spoon is the sun, on the other is the rain illustrating how blessed we are with balanced weather conditions. The heart at the centre of the spoon may be opened, triggering a musical movement of (Amazing Grace). To receive God's riches we simply need to open our hearts.

Time, a precious gift

This lovespoon has a clock movement in the centre to remind us that in today's society we need to take a moment to consider that time is such a precious gift and should be cherished more than silver and gold.

Life, a game of chance

This spoon reflects upon the topical debate of society's understanding of right and wrong. It takes the form of a roulette wheel and poses the question, is life just a game of chance? Do we just spin the wheel and leave it to fate, or do we accept Christ's invitation now?

The key to life

Is the key to life in:
- Fame or fortune?
- Scientific advances?
- Exploring space?
- Conquering diseases?
- Wealth?
- Yourself and your family?
- Or is it the cross of Christ?

We have the freedom to choose.

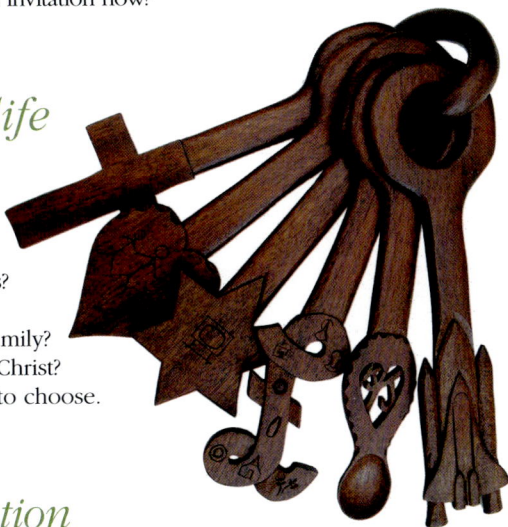

Communication

Although modern technology has seen rapid progress in communications, people still misinterpret and misunderstand one another. Often these situations can be accepted however, problems with prejudices still occur.

The trumpet, when viewed in an upright position represents the tower of Babel. The Bible states that the people of Babel were given different languages by God to prevent them from building a tower to heaven. The fish shaped bowl recalls the fact that early Christians used this as secret symbol to indicate their faith to one another. The jumbled up letters on the stave make the word communication.

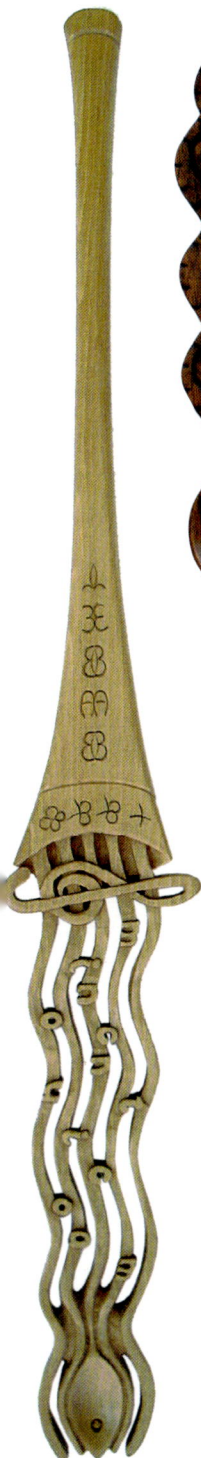

Your star will shine

When children do well in school
they often receive a star. However,
there is disappointment when they
do their best and it is not always
acknowledged. Life can appear to be
just like that. Be patient, have faith
and one day your star will shine.

Count your blessings

As the years go by sometimes it
is necessary to reflect and take
stock. The expression "Count your
blessings" comes to mind, and so
these words have been carved on
the front. The wheels in the centre
give the effect of a milometer.
Each wheel has a number of motifs
portraying some of the blessings
received in daily life.

Your word is light to my path

A path is woven through the spoon with a dragon's tail at the
base. This is used to illustrate some of the problems of life. The
pathway continues from the base to the top, where an open book
is shown with the message "Your word is a light to my path."

Celtic style lovespoons are
also popular throughout
Wales, especially the
celtic cross.

Events and O.

The new millennium was marked, by carving the date at the top of the spoon, using links. The theme for this spoon is tradition and its value. There is a place for tradition, but it is important that it does not take priority over worship. Under the links there are two crowns, one of thorns and one of traditional monarchy .In a life filled with tradition and worldly pursuits the crown which is sought is a perishable one, whereas a life filled with Christ promises an imperishable crown in heaven. Beneath the crowns sits a throne on top of the world, representing a Biblical verse "The earth is my footstool", a reminder of God's awesome power.

This spoon attempts to challenge our preconceptions. We are taught as a rule that wood floats, however this is not always true. It is made from purple heart in such a way that when placed in water, one part floats whilst the other sinks. The hope is that through Christ, our anchor, we still have a link with those who have passed away.

This spoon shows an apple with a No 11 which represents New York and The Twin Towers. Symbolizing the events of Sept.11.2001. Underneath the apple is a shell with a pearl at its centre, surrounded by the symbols of the main religions of the world.

In the shape of the letter 'V', the spoon carved from oak is a symbol of the word victory. It is a reminder of the celebrations on Trafalgar Day, but also Christ's triumph over evil. After the 7th July attacks in London, some of the first pictures showed flowers and flags being laid at the different locations. One particular flag stood out, the maple leaf of Canada .The consequence of these acts very quickly affected the whole world .The spoon has different leaves from various parts of the world, with the base of the maple leaf shaped like the dove.

The spoon has a loose seed in the stem for the birth of a child, Matthew.

Another traditional way for recording the birth of a child is by carving a link, the idea being another link in the family.

The spoon bowl represents a bell clapper, when it is lowered the word 'doubt' is visible. When it is raised the word 'faith' appears and the rings fit together making the sequence for the five Olympic rings. In this case it is the bowl of the spoon which holds the rings In position, but in life it is Gods love that holds faith in place.

Materials *for making lovespoons*

Although lovespoons were originally made from wood, today it is common to find lovespoons made from other materials such as coal, silver and chocolate. Some timbers are more suitable for carving than others. The choice of wood depends on personal preference and availability.

With the call to be vigilant in recycling materials it was decided to recycle a piece of wood from an old piano. A walnut veneer on top of tulip wood was used to form the nine and nought for the year nineteen ninety.

A branch from a local apple tree cut in the shape of a fish, caught on a hook with a cross at the top. Raises the question. What are you hooked on?

A very simple spoon shaped from a log of holly, gives an explanation for the terms 'kenetic' and 'potential energy'. An arrow set in a bow ready to be fired, has potential energy. When it is released kenetic energy is produced. Likewise the log hung on the wall has potential energy, when it is removed, revealing its other side kenetic energy is produced. Everyone has potential energy within, it is only when that potential is put into action that kenetic energy is created, hopefully for the good of mankind.

Sometimes in life we have to wait and be patient for the right moment.

The sailing ship can only move on the sea when the wind blows. To rest, wait and listen is important. This spoon was used as a prelude to the longest lovespoon.

Acknowledgements

Thanks to Kay and David White for their cottage photograph and the members of St. Elidyr Church, East Williamston for the altar photograph.

First Edition 2007

Copyright is the property of the authors and publishers K & J.A. Thomas
The Lovespoon Workshop, Inwood, Cold Inn, Kilgetty, Pembrokeshire, Wales SA68 0RP

www.lovespoons.org.uk   email. info@lovespoons.org.uk

Design and Print by Monddi Dimond Press, Pembroke SA71 4DH